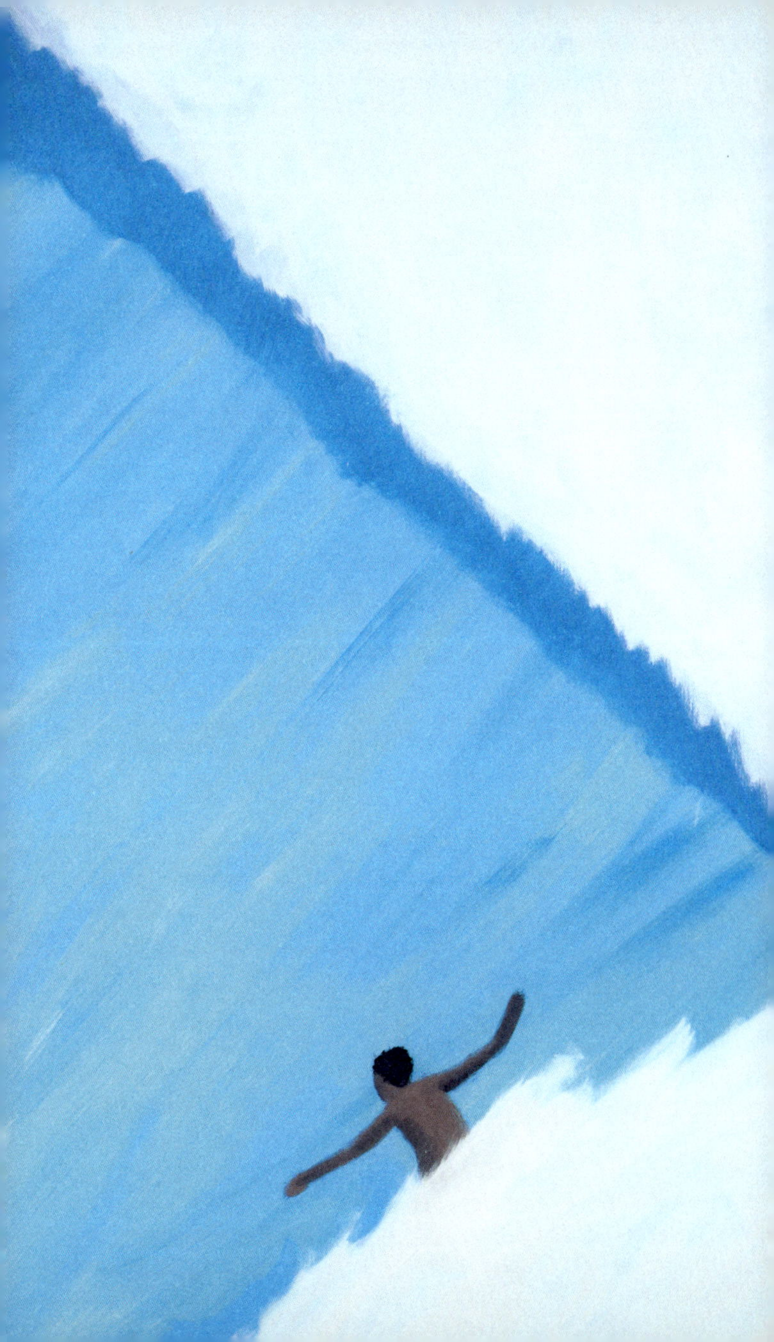

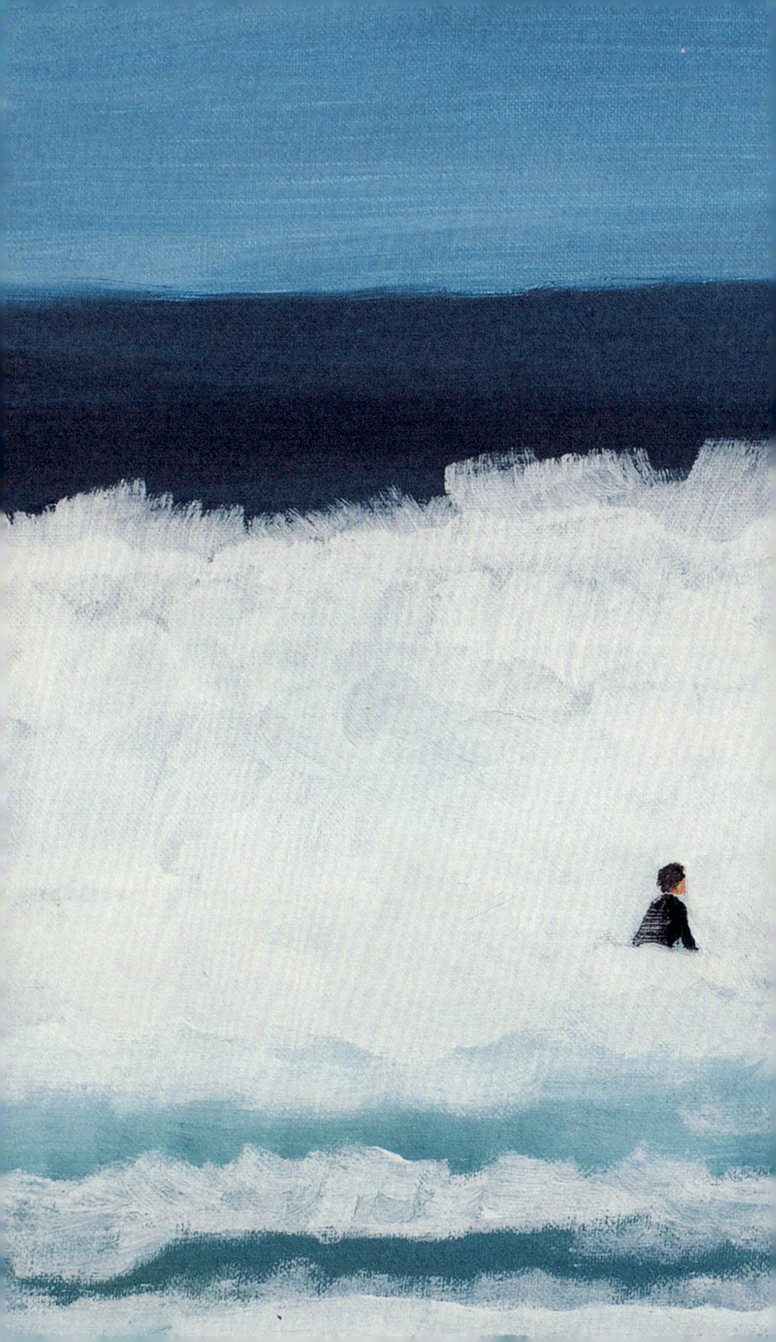

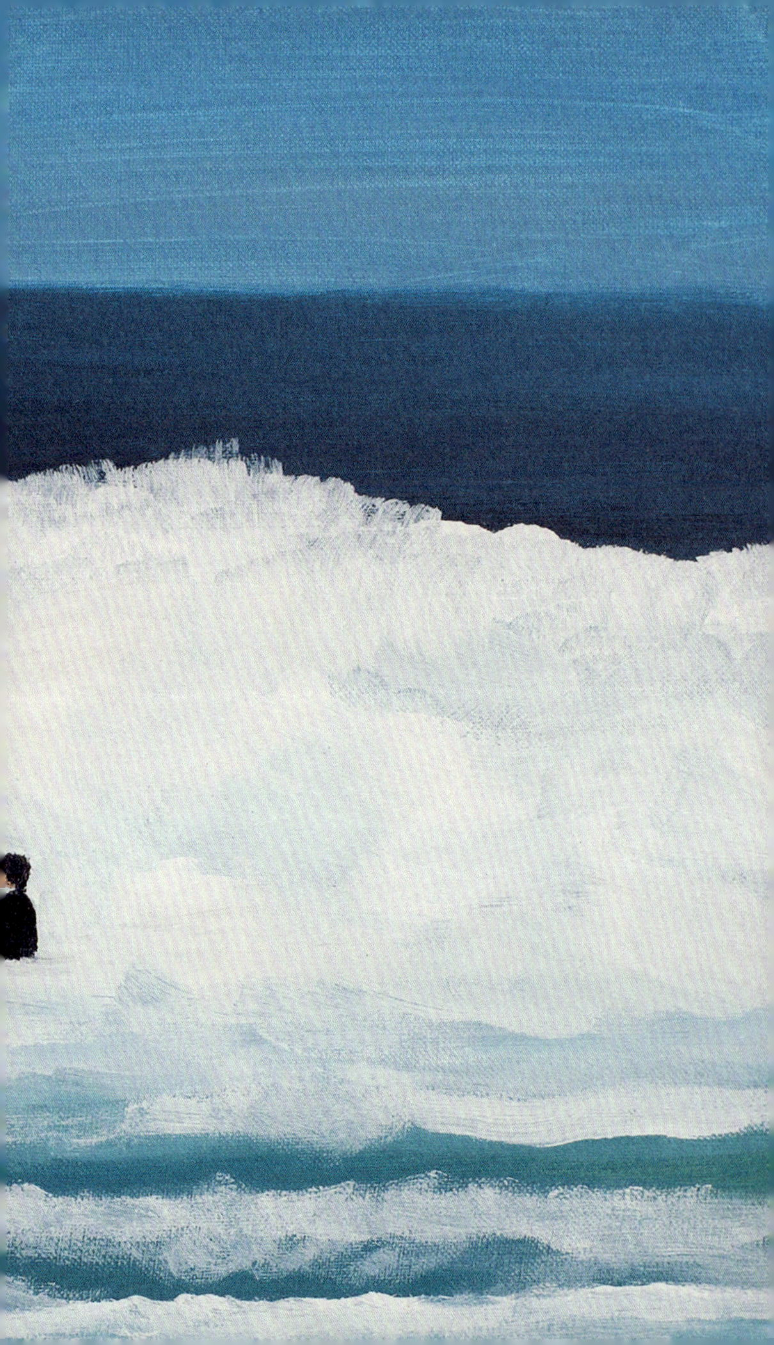

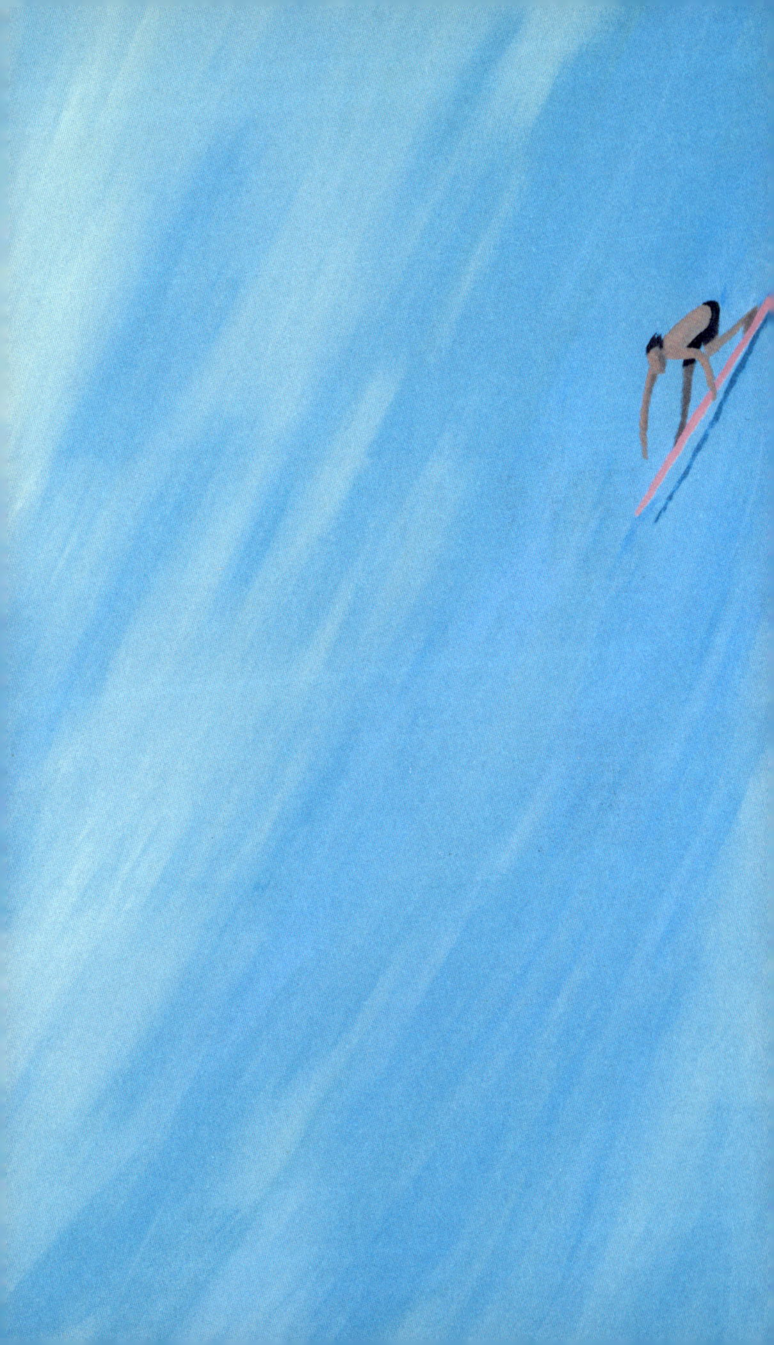

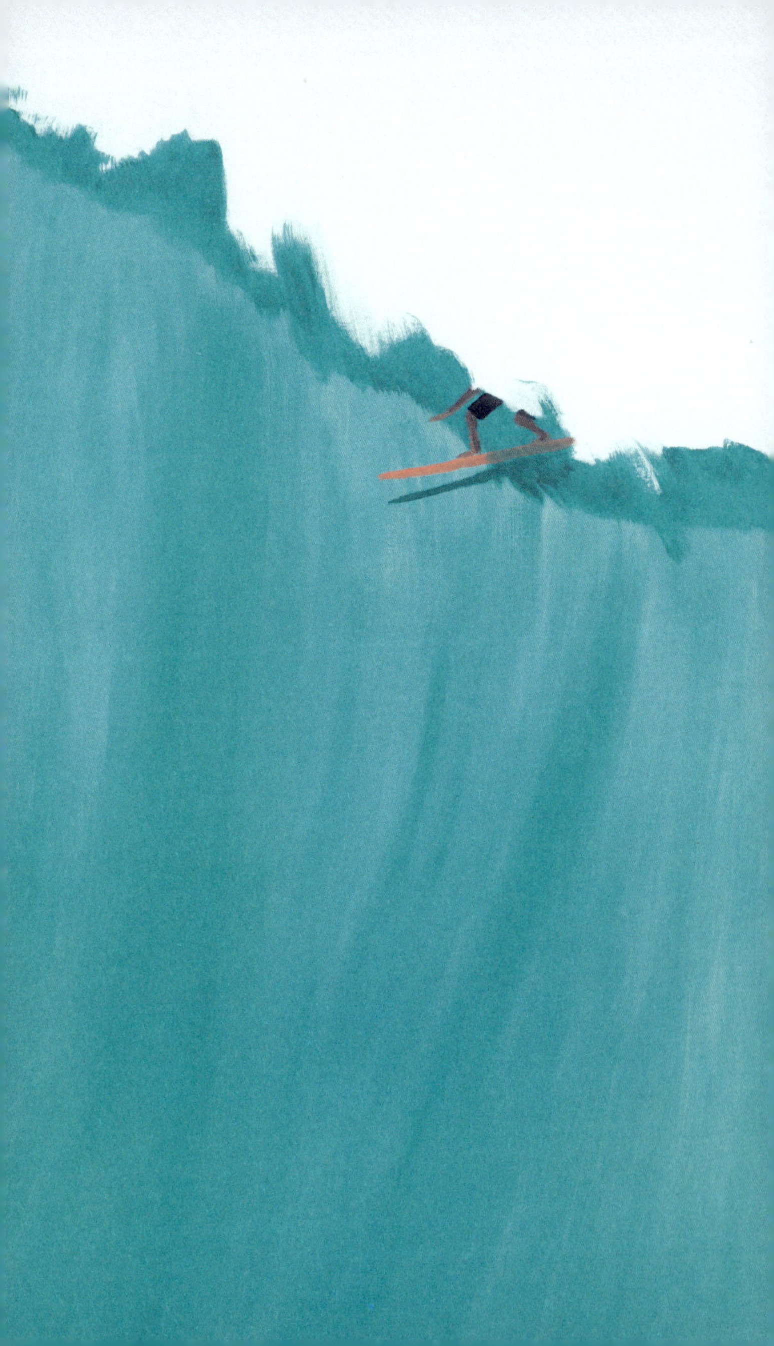

Jean Jullien
Punctuations

Cédric, Voyou, Yusuke, Hida San, Boris, Mathieu, Étienne

First Edition

Published by Nieves
www.nievesbooks.com

ISBN 978-3-907179-78-9